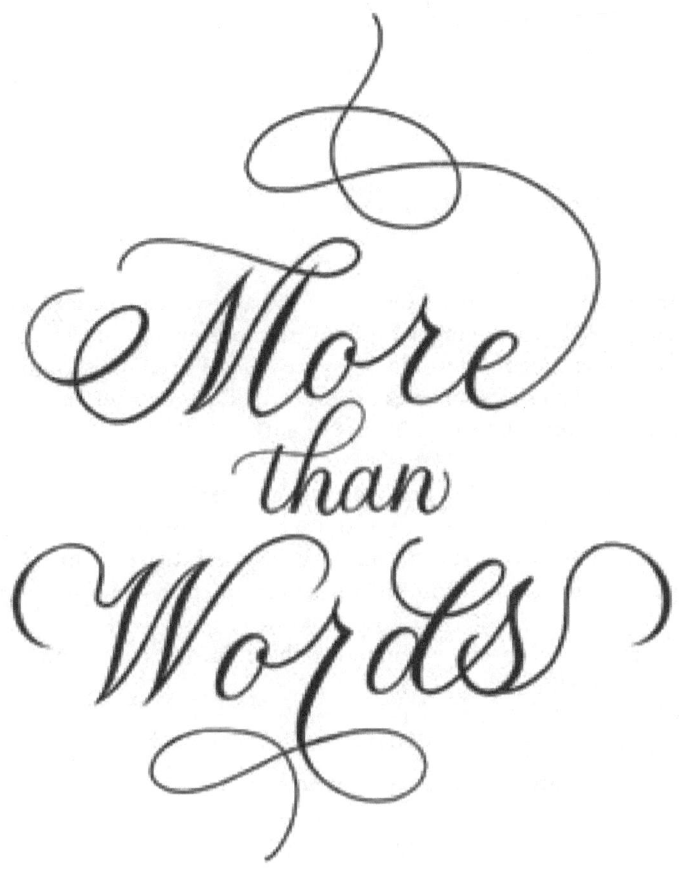

More than Words

Zack Shah

Books may be purchased by contacting the publisher and author at:
penwingspublishing@gmail.com
Cover Design: Charissa Ong Ty
Illustration: Iffah Hazirah
The Fell Types are digitally reproduced by Igino Marini.
www.iginomarini.com
Publisher: Penwings Publishing
Editor: Penwings Publishing
ISBN: 978-967-14227-3-1
1. Poetry 2. Fiction
First Edition

CONTENTS

Prologue

To love and pain
    and sadness too,
    to life in all
    its changing hue.

From crimson blush
    to shades of blue,
    I dedicate these words
    to you.

PART I

Sweet Nothings

Melancholia

Joy is but a fleeting shadow
    misery, a bore.
    Happy endings, mere fairy tales
    fictitious to the core.

Life is but a string of moments
    a never-ending chore,
    each passing day as pointless
    as the days that came before.

Love is our only respite
    a golden gleam amidst the grey,
    a sliver of the sun's warm light,
    on a cloudy winter day.

Forget Me Not

You've always had a bad memory my dear,
    but I adored you despite,
    all the birthdays and anniversaries
    that you've forgotten.

Maybe that was why
    we ended things,
    ours was a romance,
    misbegotten.

I reminded you:
    think of me always,
    remember me,
    forget me not.

Alas, of all the loves
    you've ever had,
    I was the first
    that you forgot.

Blue devils

I'm depressed again
    for no reason,
    and I don't know why.

It's okay,
    just let me curl up
    under my duvet, and cry.

Tsunami

I was an island
    and you were
    the sea.

And your words
    were the waves
    that engulfed
    every single
    part of me.

GREY MATTER

This fickle mind of mine
    may often wander.

To find many miscellaneous
    things to ponder.

Like forces at work
    much greater than we.

Magic and mischief
    and poetry.

But no matter how long
    or far it tries to stray.

Its thoughts of you
    will always stay.

EYE OF THE STORM

Keep me safe my dear, hold me as I fall asleep, so that I may drift into the chaos of my dreams, untouched by all the troubles raging around inside me. Let your arms be my anchor so that when I wake, with ocean foam in my lungs and a headful of hurricanes, you will always be there to pull me back to shore.

BUTTERFINGERS

You wanted me to give you the one thing
    that would prove my love was true,
    when just saying that you felt the same
    way was all you had to do.

But it slipped from your butterfingers
    and crashed to the floor and broke in two.
    I was foolish to have entrusted
    such an irreplaceable thing to you.

Now even all the king's horses
    and all the king's men,
    couldn't put my heart
    back together again.

CITY GIRL

Starlight in her soul
     sadness in her heart,
     moonbeams in her hair
     madness in her art.

Monsters in her head
     demons on her bed,
     poems on her lips
     magic on her fingertips.

Muse

I could write all I want about love,
    about setting suns and summer skies.
    When all I see in the stars above
    is the twinkle in your eyes.

I know now, beyond the shadow of a doubt
    and this much is true,
    of all the things I love to write about
    the best by far was you

INESCAPABLE

I wish I could drink,
    or cut
    or sleep
    or love the pain away.

But the monsters
    won't let me go
    and my demons love to play.

Mind Games

I followed you through moonlit paths
    and lost my way
    in the wilderness.

Tasted you in saccharine fruits
    between mouthfuls
    of bitterness.

Found you among
    the burs and thorns
    where I expected tenderness.

Never knowing that these dreams of you
    were nothing more
    than a nightmare I can't outrun.

I failed to see that I was sleeping with demons
    making love to monsters
    and swimming with sharks for fun.

EUPHORIA

Nothing like the taste
    of your sweet lips against mine:
    honey, wine and bliss.

Oh, how I long for
    a chance to savor
    once more,
    a flavor
    as exquisite as this.

Is it no wonder
    why I can't resist,
    asking for another kiss?

Slumber Party

You can dress your sadness in pretty things
    or paint it faceless,
    cover it in flowers
    if that helps you sleep better at night.

But it'll always be there before you go to bed,
    to tuck you in, to hold you tight
    to keep you company
    'till morning light.

QUESTION

Baby,
    I don't need you to tell me
    you love me
    every time I ask.

What I want you to do
    is spell out the answer
    on my neck
    with your tongue.

Sweet Nothings

Tender whispers
    loving words,
    spoken softly,
    in my ears,
    of future dreams
    and yesteryears,
    with stolen kisses
    here and there
    and silly games
    of truth or dare.

To pass the time
    at break of day
    or while the silent
    nights away
    until the second
    we must part
    with tired lips
    and heavy hearts
    to meet once more
    upon our bed
    with all the words
    we left unsaid.

VALENTINE

I have a box of chocolates
    on the coffee table,
    and a trashy romance
    on the nightstand.

You can keep your roses and poems
    and your less-than-average
    late-night plans.

For the lovelorn souls
    you can't wait
    to screw.

Enjoy it while you can my dear,
    because for me,
    this Valentine's Day
    a glass of wine will do.

Fortune Cookies

False and pleasant foretellings concealed
    within a wholesome disguise.

The taste of which, I once loved,
    but have now come to despise.

Just when I thought, you meant every word,
    imagine my surprise.

Your promises remind me
    of fortune cookies, my dear;
    hollow, sweet and full of lies.

Wishful Thinking

There are places I wish I'd been,
   memories I wish I'd made.

Moments I wish I'd lived,
   people I wish had stayed.

Things I wish I'd done,
   and wishes that don't come true.

I wonder why it is I'm still wishing,
   for these things I never knew.

Lost Cause

You filled my eyes with starlight
    sprinkled moondust in my hair,
    although you filled my heart with delight
    you could not silence my despair.

You filled me once with hope
    you filled me once with wonder,
    though you calmed the storm that raged inside
    you could not tame the thunder.

There was nothing you could do my love
    for I was beyond salvation, you see
    so all I can do now is thank you
    for trying to save what was left of me.

DAMAGED GOODS

A shattered soul
   a broken mind,
   parts and pieces
   left behind.

Half a life
   nothing more,
   when I arrived
   on your front door.

You took me in
   and glued me back,
   made me whole
   and hid each crack.

Despite how I cringed
   at my reflection,
   you learned to love
   each imperfection.

When hating my flaws
   was all that I knew,
   you taught me
   how to love them too.

All or Nothing

Let me be the wind in your lungs,
    the sunlight that dances on your skin,
    all the songs that
    fill your ears.

I just want to be the gold in your hair,
    the blue in your eyes,
    the red in your blood
    and the salt in your tears.

Let me be the sound of your heart,
    the whispers of your lips
    and the poems that you love to hear.

Tell me, is all this
    too much
    to ask
    my dear?

HANDLE WITH CARE

I can shatter from a mere ripple,
    I can scatter from a single breeze.

I can disintegrate from a puff of breath,
    I can break from the smallest sneeze.

But all in all I must confess, there is a threat,
    much greater to my fragility than these.

Promise me something my love,
    if only to put my mind at ease.

My heart bruises from a single touch,
    so be gentle with it please.

Hornet's Nest

There are just some words
    that are better left unsaid,
    no matter how fresh they are
    on the tongue.

Because memories are a can of worms
    with a half-closed lid,
    just waiting to be sprung.

Don't poke around a hornet's nest
    unless you want to get stung.

So for now, let's leave reminiscences
    to the foolish, the restless
    the unrepentant and the young.

Happy Place

When I have lost all that I own
    but these words that I so cherish,
    may I subsist on them alone
    if all the world should perish.

And if ever when this Earth should be
    as dark and damned as seventh hell,
    may I still have my poetry
    may I be forever under its spell.

Guilty Pleasure

Secret thoughts
    in crowded streets,
    of naughty things
    and sweat-stained sheets,
    of citrus pies
    and chocolate sweets,
    and cupboards full
    of hidden treats.

But between hiding innuendoes
    in cryptic metaphors,
    sniffing pages
    in old bookstores,
    and living vicariously
    behind closed doors,
    there is nothing else
    that I enjoy more,
    than the thought of how
    my skin would feel
    on yours.

PART II

Pretty Lies

Best Mistake

I can't say I regretted nothing
    because I sometimes think about
    what we had.

About all the moments and memories
    we shared, both the good times
    and the bad.

And although I know I should
    embrace my circumstances
    and accept them as they are.

I must confess, of all the mistakes
    I've ever made
    you were, my dear,
    the best by far.

Venom and Nectar

You were both
    honey and poison,
    venom and nectar,
    frost and heat.

Loving you my dear
    is a pleasant pain,
    a bitter victory,
    a happy defeat.

Every time you flowed
    through my veins,
    my suffering,
    my love,
    would always be sweet.

Here be Nightmares

Sometimes it's not the ghosts
    beneath our beds, that torment us
    every night,
    but the secrets that we keep.

We carry these things inside of us
    that make us crawl
    beneath the sheets
    and weep.

They dwell inside our dreams
    like phantoms,
    they haunt us in our sleep.

There be Monsters

Make peace with your horns
    with your bloodlust and
    blood-red eyes,
    with your green skin and
    rows of razor sharp teeth.

Because to be rid of the ugly,
    terrifying parts of your soul
    is something mere wishing
    won't fulfil.

Make peace with the voices that won't stop until
    the wolf inside has had its fill,
    because the beast in your head
    won't rest 'till your dead.

Once Bitten

There was a time I would recall
    the darkest in my mind,
    when I had walked into the fire
    with both eyes blind.

With my head full of hope
    and my heart on the line,
    when I had what I wanted
    but life had been unkind.

I have tasted the flame
    and gotten burned,
    a cautionary tale
    of a love that was spurned.

A lesson in recklessness,
    the cruellest I have learned.

TWICE SHY

A crime I've not forgiven,
    a memory I can't forget.

A chance I once had taken,
    that I've now come to regret.

But the clock would not turn back for me,
    and time will not rewind.

Falling in love is risky business,
    as you will soon come to find.

So remind yourself before all else,
    of all the ones that you have yearned.

That all the feelings you have kept,
    matter not unless returned.

Pretty Lies

Tell me my dear why should I believe what you say
    when the ones who leave once swore to stay
    when things end even before they've begun?

Why should I trust you when I have been told
    that at the end of every rainbow there's a pot of gold
    when truly there are none?

Between ever afters and happy endings
    soulmates and silver linings
    and other promises that your sweet lips have spun.

Why should I listen to what you whisper in my ear
    when you're telling me all the things I want to hear
    illusions that will one day come undone?

But I must confess of all the times you gave your word
    and all the lies that I have heard
    forever was my favourite one.

The Ugly Truth

How can you still say we're fine
    when you've ignored all the signs
    in a world where nothing is as what it seems.

Between the World Wide Web and the 8pm news,
    a virtual universe of wonder and abuse
    where tragedy is turned into memes.

Where facts are cherrypicked, sugarcoated and paraphrased
    where the gory details are edited and erased
    and music is used to drown out the screams.

In a world of fake smiles and crocodile tears
    where the truth is not always pleasant to hear
    where all we have are our dreams...?

Gilded Cage

Gleaming bars
    of solid gold,
    a prison built
    against the cold,
    a world of wonders
    to behold,
    that eyes can see
    but hands can't hold.

Will I fly
    and learn to sing
    or will I let them
    clip my wing?

Bittersweet

That bitterness in your mouth
    the honey on your lips,
    the sickening delight of tasting
    your savoury fingertips.

Your kisses as sweet as candy
    your breath, the smell of wine,
    what a pleasant torment this must be
    to feel your tongue on mine.

HOUSE OF CARDS

Arguing with you
    is a tricky endeavour.

An art which
    I rarely dabble in, if ever.

But I will promise
    to keep my balance
    around you
    as well as I am able.

Because our love my dear
    is like a house of cards
    precariously stacked
    on a very wobbly table.

MAKEOVER

I have decided that I will cover all
   the ugly parts of my life
   with beautiful things.

Dress my demons in the finest silk
   embroider over my heart
   with gold and silver thread
   and drape over my sorrows
   a blanket of roses.

Holy Grail

I searched for you
    in sacred caves,
    in cursed tombs
    and haunted graves,
    through hidden riddles
    and secret rhymes,
    through puzzles and clues
    of ancient times.

But in all the luck
    that chance begets
    I found you amongst
    my past regrets.
    When at last I partook
    of your golden lip,
    and drank of forevers
    from that single sip,
    I learned that an eternity
    with you, however brief,
    had all indeed been
    worth my grief.

If Only

I discovered that I enjoyed
     torturing myself
     for lack of better things
     to do.

Indulging in daydreams
     that will leave me
     oftentimes feeling
     a little blue.

But of all the torments
     I most enjoyed,
     that would always make
     my heart rue.

Were thoughts of what
     we could have been
     if you had said
     "I love you, too."

Late Bloomer

Sleeping leaves,
    tight curled
    petals shut,
    against the world,
    where other flowers
    have long unfurled.

She wakes half-formed -
    the last to bloom,
    in a sea of rivals
    starved of room.
    For her, the winter
    comes too soon.
    By death of spring
    she waits her doom.

Wonder Drug

You once swore to soothe my anguish,
  to bring me peace of mind.

To be the medicine that I've been needing,
  the remedy I could not find.

So I drank your words and swallowed your kisses,
  as through my lips your lies were poured.

You fed me a song with a spoonful of sugar,
  and promised me that I was cured.

But it was all a clever scheme,
  and the hope you sold was just a dream.

Black Magic

Midnight eyes
    light with stars,
    fingers filled
    with deviltry.

A voice that could
    melt mountains,
    lips adrip
    with poetry.

Whatever it is
    you're doing to me,
    I swear it's some kind
    of wizardry.

Teach me some of that
    old-school voodoo that you do
    and baby, I can show
    you some witchery.

Guardian Angels

I've never been the spiritual type, but meeting you made me question everything I thought I knew about the existence of the divine, whether our encounter was planned by fate. Some people, I realized didn't need to have pearl white wings or a halo. A heart of gold is sometimes all it takes for a person to save someone from destroying themselves.

And just when I thought I was damned for good, you wrenched me out from the depths of my hell and taught me that salvation was as simple as forgiving myself. From that day on I believed in the possibility of a higher power.

Make Believe

I am quite unlovable you see,
    and this is true I'm afraid.

But I am adored and cherished, however,
    in all the little games I've played.

In the many lives I've lived,
    through the many books I've read.

In all the imaginary worlds that I've conjured,
    that come alive inside my head.

And yes it might be a little tragic,
    and maybe a little sad,

But the dreams in which I was in love
    were the best I've ever had.

Daydreams

There is a hunger deep inside
    a thirst I wish to slake.

To soothe a yearning long ignored
    and ease this lovelorn ache.

Alas there are urges we must forgo,
    and deeds we should forsake.

In the place of all the little fantasies
    in which we oftentimes partake.

These thoughts of you that fill my mind
    a magic spell that I can't break.

How strange it is to dream of you
    even when I'm wide awake.

Irony

How considerate of the world
    to supply us
    with a thousand ways
    to numb ourselves
    from a thousand sufferings
    that it's left
    on our doorstep.

Denial

Ever think about the lies
    adults tell you
    when you were a child?

Now that you're one of them,
    do you find yourself
    telling the same lies
    to yourself?

Reality Check

A life I used to live
    in gladness,
    a realm within
    the looking glass.

A world of wonders
    and delight,
    that I always thought
    would last.

To leave these fantasies
    where they are,
    in the bowels
    of my past.

Please let me stay
    another night, my dear,
    that is all
    I ask.

Creature Comforts

A bed of roses
    made for me,
    a nest to call my own.

Loving words
    as warm as fire,
    to melt a heart of stone.

A pair of arms
    to wrap me 'round,
    in case I feel alone.

Oh, how wonderful
    it would be to have,
    these things I've never known.

Hearts of Stone

A girl who gave her all to he,
    who tore her fragile heart in three.

A boy who sold his soul to be with she,
    who danced upon his grief with glee.

They told themselves right there and then,
    to never fall in love again.

Either Or

It may sound like a blessing,
    it may seem like a curse.

But there is no equal to or lesser than
    with love, and the same is true in reverse.

It's either the best thing
    that's ever happened to you,
    or the worse.

KINDERED SPIRITS

A bond between us set by fate,
    through love and hope
    and dark despair.

That nothing in this cruel world
    to which I can compare.

How odd it seems to me at least
    these traits we seem to share.

Through all the trials that life has dealt,
    I have to say,
    the two of us make quite the pair.

BAD HABITS

A cigarette or two, a glass of wine, or three,
    to numb the wounds that we can't see.

Smelling sounds and tasting sights,
    to while away our listless nights.

Making love on strangers' beds,
    to soothe the monsters in our heads.

To those who deem our deeds profane,
    sadness leaves no room for shame.

Oxygen

Take my breath away, completely and all at once.
Don't steal my air in bits and pieces, drown me in
one smooth move and leave me dead, so I won't lie
there, like a fish out of water, gasping for you to
blow life back into my lungs.

RESCUE ME

Someone please rescue me,
    from this mediocre life
    where all I have,
    is the torment of my own desires
    and endless days,
    of being alone with my thoughts.

Writer's Block

Must this be how I fare,
    when life itself has struck me dumb?

When I used to type without a care,
    'till my fingers go quite numb.

Unless I find a way, if I so dare,
    to reuse each precious crumb.

All that's left for me to do is stare,
    for words that may never come.

When all my answers lie elsewhere,
    at the tip of someone else's thumb.

PART III

Love Story

More than Words

Anything can be passed off as poetry these days
    a kiss on the forehead,
    sweet nothings,
    teardrops,
    a love letter.

But the way you looked at me that day,
    was more than words could ever say.

Never Again

Of all the dreams that I could dream,
   there was always one
   that would inspire,

A fear greater than those
   of beasts or darkness
   of death by fire,

But at times I ponder my desire
   the likes of which I can't compare,

A voice would tell me: "Do it"
   when all others screamed "Beware"

I find that love is too much a risk,
   in this game where the odds
   are never in your favor
   and the rules were never fair,

So I told my guardian angels
   and all the lesser devils
   I'd rather tell the truth,
   then accept their foolish dare.

All that Glitters

You looked for gold in a diamond mine,
   and cursed the gems you left behind,
   not knowing that there were other things
   of better worth
   on this earth,
   as you will soon come to find.

Precious things don't always shine.

HEAD OVER HEELS

I remember how you used to
     take my breath away
     the way you'd
     make me blush.

The way you'd make me sweat
     profusely,
     and the way my blood would rush.

At the thought of seeing you again
     or just by having you around.

Just when I thought my world
     couldn't get any more confusing
     when everything was upside down.

All I needed to do was remind myself
     about what I already knew.

And that was I had already fallen
     head over heels,
     in love with you.

Ashes to Ashes

Scorch me with your kisses,
    burn me with your breath,
    leave me lingering in between
    the throes of life and death.

Save me from the flames
    my love, but fill me with desire,
    for you are the kindling
    baby, and I am the fire.

Dust to Dust

We look for signs where there are none,
    sending prayers to an empty sky.

Earthbound creatures chained by fate,
    wishing we could fly.

To live and hope and want and hurt,
    and never know the reason why.

Most will toil through all their days,
    and watch their dreams go by.

Some will never fall in love,
    and some are dead before they die.

Full Circle

The ups and downs
    I shared with you,
    through all the years that span.

A rollercoaster ride
    that we endured,
    with all my heart within your hand.

It hurts me so to take it back
    when ending things,
    was never in the plan.

It's sad to meet again
    as strangers,
    to end where we began.

Baggage

We carry so much these things
   handed to us by fate,

It's a wonder how we've not
   crumbled from the weight.

Sinking Ship

You cannot claim to know of death
    until the day you hold your breath,
    should all the waters reach your knees
    when storms have raged your seven seas.

And when the darkness takes its toll
    and chains an anchor to your soul,
    what else is there to do but drown
    when the only way to go is down.

Deep Waters

Of all the terrors in have faced,
   there is none quite so grim.

As the darkness that has me bowed,
   to its every twisted whim.

Filling my soul with an ocean of tears,
   'till it is filled to the brim.

I can't drown my demons my dear
   they've taught themselves to swim.

Rabbit Hole

Chasing shadows, catching mist
    to dream of things that don't exist,
    to delve in depths you can't unlearn
    beyond the point of no return,

And take the path where it may go
    where all your fears can shrink and grow,
    what else is there to do but flee
    for in my hand I hold the key,

To unlock a land of stranger things
    and all the wonder that it brings,
    where fairies, demons, ghosts and sprites
    indulge me with unique delights.

Where thoughts can fly and flutter free
    and answers lie in cups of tea,
    to stay awhile or never leave
    within the lure of this reprieve.

If should the truth I fail to find
    it matters not to lose my mind,
    for I have learned of its appeal
    and I am lost to all that's real.

Smoke and Mirrors

Beware the wizard and his wand,
    for with a flick your heart is gone.

He'll conjure flowers from his gloves,
    and turn your terror into doves.

He'll seal your lips and take your words,
    and turn your wishes into birds.

He'll pull a promise out of his hat,
    and give you nothing else but that.

He'll steal your heart through sleight of hand,
    so run away while you still can.

Beware the wizard's evil kiss
    for with a snap your heart is his.

Something Wicked

Beware my dears of the monsters
   and the undead.

Of the demons and ghosts
   that hide beneath your bed.

In a world of darkness filled
   with horrors and dread.

Where only the stuff of
   nightmares is bred.

If you think love is a risk worth taking,
   remember this instead.

Fools rush in where angels fear to tread.

Unfinished Business

Shadows dancing on the walls
    phantom voices in the halls,
    unseen arms that hold me tight
    the things that keep me up at night.

Your imprint on my empty bed
    the shades of you that won't stay dead,
    the memory that haunts my room
    that won't remain within its tomb.

Footsteps walking up the stairs
    faces lurking here and there,
    the echoes that your whispers make
    the ghost of you that keeps me awake.

Open Book

Hearts on sleeves, wounds laid bare
    the pleasant masks we sometimes wear,
    to hide our secrets where they dwell
    except from those who know us well.

How painful it must be to bleed
    your deepest thoughts for all to read,
    in every page where they reside
    but in this way, I can confide,

So look beyond the tattered binding
    to find all that I have been hiding,
    and maybe learn a thing or two
    from all the clues I left for you.

Shades of Grey

To question all of life's charades,
    and see through its disguise.

To look beyond its many shades,
    through bright and brand new eyes.

You'll see that love is not as black and white,
    as one would first surmise.

How quaint it is to unsettle,
    those who deem the deed unwise.

And yet view the world as good or evil
    or indifferent in their eyes.

Love and Loss

The words they said
    still rung through me,
    as I reminisced
    that fateful day.

Of the one who broke
    my heart and left,
    even though
    he swore to stay.

To those who told me
    that it was worth it,
    this is what
    I have to say.
    I'd rather not
    have loved at all,
    than to have loved and lost
    this way.

FORBIDDEN FRUIT

Golden apples
    on trees of thorn,
    a garden where
    dark things are born.

This sweet temptation
    before my eye,
    the taste of which
    I can't deny.

Dangling, swaying
    hanging low,
    a flavour that
    I yearn to know.

A fleeting glance
    a tempting sight,
    to take the chance
    and steal a bite.

A mouthful there
    a nibble here,
    they say "beware"
    or so I fear.

The briefest bliss
    from deep within,
    how sweet it is
    indeed to sin.

Tongue Tied

No amount of poetry
  can explain how I feel
  and I am bereft of rhymes.

But I do confess
  simple words
  work best sometimes.

And even though you have taken
  all my sentences away
  I do have one thing left to say:

Of all the words that I have said
  and all the songs
  that I have sung,

There is nothing quite like the taste,
  of how your name
  rolls of my tongue.

NEVERLAND

Let shadows play
    in dead of night,
    and fly us off
    by morning light,
    to lands beyond
    the sea and sky,
    where souls and dreams
    can never die,
    with pixie dust
    and pure belief
    away from all
    the pain and grief,
    to play with fairies
    and mermaids too,
    in mountain mist
    and rivers blue,
    where we will then
    forever spend,
    'till time itself
    has met its end.

Old Flame

The kiss you left upon my lips,
    that burns me to this day.

The imprint of your fingertips,
    that never goes away.

The embers of my desire,
    that makes you so hard to forget.

I've become too fond of the fire,
    to extinguish you just yet.

LOVE STORY

Our story starts
    with shy hellos,
    with smitten hearts
    and crimson rose.
    My hand in yours
    and yours in mine
    as stars and moons
    above align,
    making love
    and butting heads,
    making up
    in hotel beds,
    through summer heat
    and winter chill
    through tear-filled eyes
    and false pretence,
    in sad goodbyes
    our story ends.

Influence

You are the waves that pull me under
    the moon that moves my tide,
    the lightning to my thunder
    the storm that stirs inside.

How can I resist your sway,
    when you're with me every day,
    when there's nowhere I can hide?

Distraction

Love is not always about the all-consuming romance they tell you about in movies. It's not always about selflessly bartering your heart out for another's. Most of the time, love is finding someone to distract you from hating yourself.

Tempus Fugit

The fleeting days
    and wilting flowers,
    the empty seconds
    and passing hours,
    that leave me restless
    day and night,
    of moments gone
    at speed of light,
    I fear one day
    I'll wake with tears,
    regretting all
    my wasted years,
    to wish for time,
    to turn around
    and even as
    I write this down
    life is slipping
    through my hand
    like microscopic
    grains of sand,
    now all I do
    is sit and sigh
    and watch the minutes
    pass me by.

ALL THE DIFFERENCE

I kept trying to convince myself
    that I was fine,
    that I could go my entire life
    without ever finding
    happiness or true love,
    that other people could
    and have survived on less.

But existing is one thing
    and to be alive,
    is something else entirely.

THICK AND THIN

I will love you my dear,
    through sleet and snow
    come hell or high water.

Through rain and shine
    through thick and thin,
    through terror and disaster.

Even when the world goes up in flames
    I will stay by your side,
    no matter the weather.

I promise I'll be with you
    if you promise me we'll brave through
    the doom and gloom together.

True Love

I look for you, where you might be,
    in glancing eyes and strangers' faces.

In passing cars and photographs,
    in wonderful and terrifying places.

Alas, my search has bore no fruit,
    and now I dream of hopeless things.

Of forehead kisses and morning texts,
    of wedding bells and wedding rings.

Will I ever find true love I wonder,
    even if it is too good to be true.

The truth is I may never know,
    but I hope one day I do.

Happy Ending

Do not tell me of happy endings my dear,
    for I do not wish for this to end.

Our story is still being written,
    and we have the rest of forever to spend.

So for now, let our ever after go on,
    through all our fleeting days.

Let's see what fate has planned for us
    and leave the rest to come-what-mays.

ACKNOWLEDGEMENTS

An ocean of gratitude to Charissa, without whom, this book would remain a tattered manuscript tucked away in a dusty corner of my closet never to see the light of day, or rather, a collection of Microsoft word documents stored on the hard drive of my laptop.

To my poor heart for putting up with so much throughout the years and helping keep every secret, feeling and sensation safe for me until the time came to give all of it away.

To the omnipotent cosmic forces who conspired to set a series of events in motion that led to me getting this book out into the world for everyone to read.

Lastly, to my family and friends, even though none of you knew anything about what I was up to.

About the Author

Zack Shah has been a lover of the written word ever since he can remember, reading fairytales and escaping ever so often into the world of make-belief, where wishes can come true with the wave of a wand and a magic spell. Growing up, he always believed that there was something magical about rhymes, about how witches and wizards would use them to reshape reality, grant everlasting life and sway the elements themselves to their whims.

While his own poems don't have that kind of power, he likes to think they carry their own kind of magic, something, deeper, darker and undeniably more human. More than Words brings to life these ideas in a haunting collection of poetry and prose, where nightmares and daydreams go hand in hand.

MORE FROM PENWINGS PUBLISHING

MIDNIGHT MONOLOGUES
By Charissa Ong Ty

No.1 Best-Selling English Poetry and Short Stories is sold in major bookstores in Malaysia, Singapore, and the Philippines.

#MidnightMonologues is divided into four parts: LOST, FOUND, HOPE, and Short Stories. In an age of decreased readership and short attention spans, this book aims to ignite the readers' imagination; with short, melodious writing.

Ebook available on Amazon Kindle:
http://amzn.to/2AHkNzT

QUESTIONS TO OUR ANSWERS
By Timothy Joshua

#QTOA is a poetry and fiction book containing three main chapters, centred around questions one would ask during different stages of a relationship: What are we? Where are we going? How are we getting there?

The poems, juxtaposed with short stories, take readers on a deeply reflective journey as they contemplate the deepest thoughts and hopes they carry for their past and present relationships.

Ebook available on Amazon Kindle:
http://amzn.to/2ncM8Hz

DAYLIGHT DIALOGUES
By Charissa Ong Ty

Back by popular demand, Charissa Ong Ty's second Poetry and Short Stories book re-explores heartbreak, deep aspirations of love, self-actualization and fictional short stories.

Pushing her boundaries with more challenging technical poetry writing, she hopes her readership would appreciate Daylight Dialogues as much as they did Midnight Monologues.

Ebook will be available on Amazon Kindle at the end of 2019.

What does my name mean?
By Charissa Ong Ty

#WDMNM is written for Gen-Ys and X-ers who are still self-actualizing. This family-friendly book can also be enjoyed by readers of all ages. This interactive, motivational, and personalized book aims to reframe thoughts about oneself as well as stresses the importance of finding one's self-identity and role in this world. "What does My name mean?" also addresses the failures and darkness one faces in a safe light, also rarely discussed in this generation.

Personalize your copy at:
 www.amazingfables.com

www.ingramcontent.com/pod-product-compliance
Lightning Source LLC
Chambersburg PA
CBHW020126180726
47992CB00020B/2520